ABC'S OF SPEAKING SUCCESS

When You Want to Connect, Clarify and Inspire Your Audience

ANNIE MEEHAN - CSP

ABC's of Speaking Success

ISBN 979-8-9860054-3-0

CONTENTS

DEDICATION

This book is dedicated to the Dreamers, Believers, Darers and Doers of this world.

Those that have a vision and pursue it into their reality.

Those entrepreneurs that complete what they set out to do because their purpose is beyond themselves, they share their stories, teach their lessons and live their dreams.

FOREWORD

This book started as a way to support business owners, entrepreneurs, franchise owners, Speakers and those dreaming of launching their own business.

I have known the challenges of owning a business for over 20 years and also know it can be lonely maybe even overwhelming at times.

So, I created this video series, which turned into a blog, which turned into a presentation, which became this book to encourage, inspire and activate business owners.

Pick a letter a day to focus on with your team, remind yourself and your organization that it all starts with A for a great Attitude no matter the circumstances.

I hope you find nuggets and tools to use as you go through this book. As your journey in your business unfolds from speaking to sales something for everyone...Wishing you Exceptional Success.

A

Is for Attitude

HOW IS YOUR ATTITUDE?

Your attitude is something you have a choice about and it is something you can control. Unfortunately, you cannot control a lot of things about business, especially when growing your own business and working for yourself. Sometimes different things pop up when you aren't prepared because it was something you never imagined. You may also feel overwhelmed with rejection at times. Your attitude, however, is something you always control. It is something you can decide before you even get out of bed in the morning.

If you choose to allow your attitude to be based

on what happens to you throughout the day, your attitude will be up and down. Ideally the kind of attitude you'll have for the day is a positive attitude no matter what the weather is like, what sort of news you find out, what good or bad things happen. If you choose to be positive and you will have a much better chance of being successful.

In the speaking profession you cannot control how other people feel. The main reason why rejection can feel so harsh to a speaker is because it feels personal. We're selling us. We don't have a product or service. We are the product and service. So when people don't want us to speak at their conference, we can take it personally. This is when you have to decide to have a good attitude anyway. In fact, you have to decide to cheer for the person who was booked when you thought you should have received the job. When you do it's amazing what will happen over the long haul.

If you keep a positive attitude no matter what the outcome of your work is, then your work will ultimately pay off. It may not be the first time, maybe not even the fourth time, but eventually it will be your turn. Continue to do the hard work with a positive attitude. When people see you being positive and encouraging for others who got the position you wanted or got the opportunity you worked so hard for, they'll remember you. A great attitude reflects well on you and makes you shine brighter than the next time someone is looking for upbeat and inspirational content, as well as a great delivery speaker, they'll choose you.

Thus if you want to be successful remember to maintain a positive attitude. No matter what the circumstances are around you, live by choice. With that said, I encourage you to choose positivity and optimism no matter your circumstances.

B

Is for Becoming

HAVE YOU BECOME WHO YOU ARE MEANT TO BE?

Often when we start a business or begin a speaking career, we have a vision. A vision about how our work is going to impact people. We want to share this vision with others and becoming is not only knowing what topic you're good at, but also listening to the feedback from the people around you.

What did your audience or target demographic hear when you spoke or promoted your business? What do they want to hear from you? Personally, I love my comment cards. When I get them back, whether I'm speaking to an audience of hundreds or even thousands, everyone has a slightly different response on what they learned or loved about my presentation.

I do comment cards for a couple of reasons. One, I love to hear the feedback. Two, and more importantly, it reminds me what's vital for them to hear. It also reminds me what they're hearing, which surprisingly, is sometimes not exactly what you're saying. Thus becoming is being open to other people's feedback.

Feedback comes in many forms. Someone in your audience may say, "I like this, but I would love if you'd spend more time on this," or "You're great at speaking about leadership." You may also hear feedback from your customers such as, "It was important to me that you started your business here," or maybe, "What I really love about your business is the relationship I have with you."

It's truly fascinating to see what people take away from a presentation Something I have heard is that because I'm so positive people want to hear me speak more about change. People can be so negative and afraid when it comes to change. However, if we listen to those people around us, then we can actually step into becoming what people need, not just what we think they need. I encourage you to be open to and aware of what other people are looking for and listening to what they need as you go out and speak.

C̄

Is for Create Meaningful Connections

CONNECTIONS COME FROM CLEAR COMMUNICATION

Sometimes we're so busy on social media we feel like we have 5,000 friends. In reality, we might not even have two or three who we make time to develop meaningful connections.

Often I'll meet a person who will tell me they used to have good friends in high school or college or at an old job. They then continue sharing how they had kids and life got busy so they don't connect with those friends as often as they did in the past. I encourage you to go back to that time.

Yes, sometimes life is busy and we can't meet with our connections all the time. However, even if you plan something for a year from now, next quarter, or even next month, it allows you to look forward to that meaningful connection and those relationships that really matter. If we have that then we're going to feel secure, confident, and connected to the world around us. We're not going to feel so alone behind a screen, talking through social media with numbers instead of individuals.

A meaningful connection is where we look someone in the eye. We know their stories and they know ours with no judgment, but rather just a good listening ear. If needed, they may even provide some sound advice. I hope you have meaningful connections in your life. If you don't yet, then I encourage you to take the time to make them or to go back to them if you had them in your past.

Connections helps us eliminate our excuses and believe in ourselves. They give us someone else to walk alongside of us who believes in us. They make all the difference when we eliminate our excuses and make meaningful connections. I hope I've encouraged you to work on eliminating your excuses, so you can focus on living an extraordinary life.

D

Is for Decisions

CAN YOU BE DECISIVE EVEN IN DIFFICULT DECISIONS?

When we're setting a goal, we have to decide to stay committed despite any challenges we may face. For example, I signed up for a challenge in which I was going to ride my bike 500 miles over a period of time. I had only ridden four miles in my life when I signed up to ride the 500 miles, but that wasn't the only difficulty I faced. I had a friend that talked me into signing up and then she quit on me. To top it off, two weeks before the challenge was to begin somebody stole my bike.

I could have quit and some may say it just wasn't meant to be. However, I made a decision and committed to something so that is what I intended to do. We must stand by our decisions and commitments even when obstacles get in our way. We choose to show people that we've decided to be committed and then we live out whatever obstacles come so we can eventually bask in our success. So when you decide, know that I'm here to support you along the way.

E

Is for Eliminate Excuses

ARE YOU READY TO ELIMINATE YOUR EXCUSES SO YOU CAN BECOME THE EXCEPTION?

As professional speakers we strive to eliminate our excuses and turn them into reasons. For example, gym clients will say to me, "You don't understand, my family has always had diabetes. It's just the way it is. Genetically, there's no hope for me." Then I have watched those same people transform their lives. Now I realize some diseases can't be cured or reversed. But some diabetes, the type dealing with diet and exercise, can be reversed.

In the past we have had many clients at our gyms come in and start by saying, "My whole family has had diabetes, so for that reason, I will do whatever it takes to be healthy. I will work out five days a week and change my eating habits, because I don't want to be the next one on the list." In this way they took their excuse for how things have always been and as an alternative, turned it into a reason motivating them to change things in their lives. Used their family's pain as fuel to do what they could about it. Might not change everything but they are doing their part

If you rely on an excuse for why your job isn't working out or why you have the wrong boss or why your relationships don't work, I encourage you to instead turn it around and look for a reason to make things work. Take your excuse and turn it into a reason why you'll do things differently.

By doing this, you can have success in an area you maybe didn't have in the past. I encourage you to eliminate your excuses, discover your why in order to live your extraordinary life.

F

Is for Feelings

FEELINGS CAN LEAD YOU ASTRAY; ARE YOU LISTENING TO YOUR HEAD OR HEART?

Feelings are important. I'm all about feelings. In fact, I tell people, I wear my feelings on my sleeve. Please don't apologize if you get too excited or too sad about something, feelings are part of who we are. I like people that show up with emotion.

I also think feelings have to be in check and cannot exclusively define us, especially if we're going to be successful in business. There will always be someone who doesn't like you, even if everyone else loves you. Sometimes I ask the teasing question, how many compliments does it take to get rid of an insult?

For example, if an audience of 1000 people hear me speak and 999 say "You're amazing," and one person says, "You have ugly shoes," I tend to think about the insult on the way home. We have to be careful about the words we absorb and how they make us feel. Thus, feelings can be dangerous.

You have to be cautious to not let one person's opinion affect how you feel. A number of years ago, I was organizing and leading a retreat for the first time. We had lots of great speakers and activities. At the end of the retreat, there was over 100 women there and we got evaluations. Almost everybody wrote great things about what they learned and what they loved. But there was one person who wrote as anonymous saying, "I didn't like the food. I didn't like the sleeping conditions. I didn't like the speakers." I was devastated because she insulted everything about the retreat. My heart was broken and my emotions were leading. Even though I had over 100 wonderful pieces of feedback, I had this one negative.

At first, I thought maybe a friend did it because they knew I was a little nervous about pulling everything together. So, I called a couple friends. Did you fill this out? No, did you and I realized I really didn't know who had filled it out. It wasn't a friend; it wasn't a joke. I was so sad at first. I thought I wanted to put together this weekend to give this gift to somebody. I realized after allowing logic to kick in, and not just emotions, that the negative person was probably in a really sad place in their life. Maybe they were walking through something dark and they needed someone to vent it out on. I provided them the space to do that. This is why we have to be careful to not allow people's feelings and reactions define us.

You see feelings are important and we need to talk about them and express them. In an audience, however, especially the larger the audience you speak to there's always going to be someone who doesn't like you. Maybe they don't like the color of your hair or they don't like your PowerPoint, they don't like this or that. For every single negative person though there can be tons of other people that love you.

I'm not saying to ignore criticism and especially not corrective criticism, which can be helpful in making us better at our practice or with our products or services. What I am saying is do not allow those feelings to define you. Take in the information, don't let it devastate you, learn from it, and then keep moving forward. If you try to set up a business and want to be successful at business judging everything by only your feelings, will keep you from that success.

In fact, if you allow other people's feelings about you or even your feelings about how you feel that day, because it's rainy or cloudy, and you can't get you motivated to get your work done, you won't be successful. However, you should strive to let logic define your business instead of feelings. Remind yourself it doesn't matter if everyone thinks you're great or not, keep moving forward.

You can be an emotional person; you can be a passionate person. On the other hand, you also have to have logic in there. If your feelings define you, then your business will ride up and down just like your emotions. Get those feelings in check by acknowledging them, but don't let them define you. Feelings, those of other people or your own, cannot define your business. If you choose to have success in your business, then keep moving forward. I encourage you to keep believing in yourself. I believe in you and I can't wait to hear about the great success that you're having in your life.

G
Is for Giving

ARE YOU MORE FOCUSED ON WHAT YOU CAN GIVE OR WHAT YOU WILL GET?

Give more of yourself, give more generously, get involved with your community, and give back. More than anything, though, find a cause.

As speakers, we can have a lot of influence in the world. We all have different things we're passionate about. I'm not here to tell you which thing to be passionate about. In fact, I wish I could choose just one or two, but there are so many things I'm passionate about.

I think it's really important to give back to a charity so people know what you're aligned with and why you're aligned with it. Is it heart disease, cancer, AIDS, diabetes? For me it is mental health and homelessness because those things both personally affected my life or the lives of family members. Thus, I care very much about them. I think when we align with an organization to give back we remind people that life isn't just all about you.

As a brick-and-mortar owner of Snap Fitness in New Prague and Lilydale, it was really important for us to get involved in the community. We would give to the sports teams, give to the schools, give to the rotary, and give to the chamber. Not only did we give to those inside our own community but we were even giving to bigger state and global causes.

So, when you have the privilege of taking the platform and somebody wants to give an additional donation, give it to your charity or your cause. There are so many foundations out there, you don't even need to start your own to begin giving back. You just need to get affiliated with a couple of places, or even one place that touches your heart and give back, whether it's your time, your resources or both.

Furthermore, the minimum we can do to give is share a little bit of time on the platform, if allowed and appropriate at your venue, to share what we care about. This is why if you want to make an additional donation, if you're looking to give somewhere, use your social media platform to help you accomplish that goal. There are so many causes and such great need out there.

We have the privilege of being influencers as speakers. By using our platform, whether it's online or in front of our audience, to share what we're passionate about, it reminds people to get involved. We can help fuel their passions and promote generosity to encourage others to give to something they care about. I think to be successful in business, we must always be giving back.

I encourage you to think about what it is you care about and how can you give back. If you want to be successful in business, then remember, it's not all about you. It's about the difference you make and how you can give back.

H

Is for Hope

EVEN IN THE HARD THERE IS ALWAYS HOPE

Today, in the ABC's of how to grow a business we have reached the letter H, which stands for hope. Once during a week when I'd been hanging out with different speakers and doing things with National Speakers Association (NSA), I was thinking about all the people talking about their topics. Some were similar and others were on opposite ends of the spectrum. As I thought about it, I realized we all kind of sell and teach the same thing. Whether it is leadership, sales, customer service, or motivation, we're all actually selling *hope*.

I think when we realize we're all selling hope it

allows us to find a better way of doing essentially the same thing, even though we each do it a little differently. I sell people the hope that they can become the exception. I also sell them the hope that they could be outstanding in their customer service and leadership.

We hope that we can be better at sales than we were last year. We hope our attitudes can actually affect how we lead and manage other people. We hope we can learn something new, which will make our jobs better.

Hope is this thing we all need, though I'm not sure if anybody has quite enough. Hope is believing in something you don't quite yet know. Or maybe you know, but you haven't applied it yet. When we start to believe in the hope that things could actually be better—and maybe even amazing—we are more likely to succeed in our goals.

However, all people get stuck at times in their life. All of us go through seasons where we feel like, "oh, I don't know if this is working right," and "I don't know if I'm doing my best."

Bringing in a speaker can jump-start, re-energize, and re-inspire the people in your audience. Even more importantly, we can show them a new path to a hopeful way to look at and do things. If you're looking for a little bit of hope and encouragement to help change what your company is going through, then try to see it as something good rather than something to fear.

I love to come in and kick a conference with a keynote presentation or lead your staff training with encouragement and hope rather than doubt and fear. When we get stuck, our minds can take over and drag us down so rapidly that we forget to have hope that not only will things be okay, but maybe they will be better than okay. Hope is what we sell and it's an exciting thing to buy! I encourage you to look back at all your past successes and then make a list of all the things you are hopeful to see happen for yourself and your business.

I

It's Not All About YOU. Less I, More They!

THERE IS NO I IN TEAMWORK

I refers to when I first started this business—I want you to like me, I want you to hire me, or I want you to read my books. When I realized it wasn't actually all about me, it was amazing how much more successful I became. I realized it's actually about you, not about me.

In the beginning, I wanted so much for you to like me, please like me, and please pick me. You've got 20 speakers to pick from, please pick me. I want to come to your conference; I think I have a great idea. When I figured out it wasn't about me or even about your liking me but it was simply about you, then I believed I could teach you something.

I could offer you something. I could inspire, encourage, and activate you to do a few things differently or look at things differently or even act differently. I could help you realize you have more of a choice than you thought. I decided that I wanted you to like you more rather than have you like me. That is truly when I found success.

In a world where we're so busy and caught up with ourselves, we are always thinking, "I want you to pick my product, my business, my service." Sometimes we fail with this mindset.

But when we shift that "I" to "you" we begin to ask the real questions. Questions like, "What can I actually offer you? What would be the benefit of you hiring me? How could you feel more successful after you listen to me? How could you have a strategy and a plan when you walk out of the room that you didn't have when you walked in or when you got done listening to me?" We find success when we ask these kinds of questions.

It's time for us to realize that our products and services are not only about us succeeding, but they're about our customers also succeeding. When they succeed, they enjoy and value what we bring to them. I think the "I" in business means don't make it all about you. Make it about them and what you have to offer and they will feel it, they will know it, and they will want more of it. Make it about liking them, not about them liking you. I encourage you to strive for success and remind yourself, the key to success is keeping the focus on them.

J

Is for the Joy of the Journey

THE JOURNEY IS MORE ENJOYABLE THAN THE DESTINATION

When a person begins a business they plan on how they're going to arrive at success. I don't know if you ever do meet a single point of success though because you hit that point and then you raise the bar. You hit that point again and then you raise the bar more. Sometimes you don't hit that point and you get discouraged. I found to be successful is to recognize this is a journey.

Some days I'll be up and other days not so up. Some days I'll be way up and some days, not up at all. That's the whole point: It's a journey. It's also about consistency through the journey. It's not about the destination, it's about the ride and knowing that you're in it for the long haul. When you know this, then you can find joy in all the moments—the good ones, the bad ones, the challenging ones, and the wonderful ones.

As the president of NSA, Minnesota, I've been on such a journey. I thought it'd be all fun and everyone would love me. It was going to be great. However, it has been quite a journey, which has included a lot of growing and more work than I thought. There has been a lot of stretching, planning, being organized and getting into the details of things that I don't necessarily love.

The journey to a successful business is about staying committed through the highs and lows. Are you in it for the ride? Or are you just in it for the rival? For me it's the ride that makes me better every day at doing the good work I have been called to do.

I hope you enjoy the journey because it's a journey to success and of success. I encourage you to be committed to the journey, even when you don't get as far or see as much success as you anticipated. If you need help along the way, I would love to come work with you and inspire you on your journey.

K

Is for Keynote

CLIMBING THE SPEAKER LADDER DOES NOT ALWAYS LEAD TO KEYNOTES

Doesn't everyone want to be a keynote speaker? It sure seems that way to me because I often hear from a lot of people, "I want to be a keynote speaker." I like to ask those people questions such as, "Have you spoken before? How many people was it for? How did it go? How long did you speak?" I find out more and more of these people are trainers, seminar leaders, consultants, and coaches but not necessarily speakers. Of course, there's nothing wrong with that, however, I think people believe keynote speaking to be the pinnacle of the speaking business and they want that for themselves.

For myself, being a keynote speaker has worked really well. People love to have me kick off their conference because I bring energy, passion, stories, and purpose. It helps them keep the fire burning for the next couple days of their conference. I also do some breakout and occasionally a seminar or an all-day training, but my primary focus is on keynoting because that's my style. My very personality is high energy. I'm a storyteller who likes to include some lessons within a great story. Keynote speaking isn't for everybody though, which is perfectly fine.

While keynote speaking works for me, don't think it makes you less of a speaker if you don't do keynoting. If you're called to speak but you excel in a group of six to twelve people, such as for a training or retreat or all-day workshop, that's beautiful. Sometimes in speaking I think people see keynote speaking as the top of the food chain, much like in leadership roles.

Instead, we need to remember it takes different personalities and strengths to do any kind of speaking. One is not less than the other. Sometimes one gets paid a little bit more, sometimes one doesn't, but it doesn't matter. Don't try to be something only for the money. It's much better to work with the gifts you have and capitalize on how you connect with people.

It takes a tremendous amount of energy to work with audiences of thousands. Especially when you aim to have each person feel like you are talking specifically to them. If that is not your strength and you try to do it anyway, it unfortunately won't lead to more business.

You need to know what your strengths are and use them to find your success. We tend to compare ourselves to others and when somebody looks like a bright, shiny light as a keynote speaker it is tempting to try it for ourselves. We should instead strive to know our own gifts and strengths and work within those.

I hope that you won't see keynote speaking as the only king in the world of speaking. There are many opportunities, many great stories, and endless lessons to learn. I encourage you to capitalize on what you're great at so your audience benefits the most from your teaching. Remember there's a place for all of us in this business so get out there and share your story.

L

Is for Love Your Clients

WHEN YOU LOVE YOUR AUDIENCE YOU WASH AWAY YOUR NERVES

I recently watched the movie Love Actually. It starts with a narrative discussing how love in the world still exists and an airport is a place we can see people's love for each other, because "love actually is all around." Yet the whole movie goes through how complicated and confusing love can be because it can be recanted. Similarly, if we don't show love to our clients, then they may recant their love for our business.

I think as a speaker, or as a business owner, you should genuinely love your clients. If you do honestly care about your clients, whether it's the one that hires you or the one that has no influence to hire you, you must care about the people in the audience. People don't remember what we say but they do remember how we make them feel.

It's true, because as a gym owner for all those years I remember the clients would come back again and again and refer their friends. They would say, "I always feel so welcome here. I always feel so heard and cared about." When you love people and make them feel special and show them they matter people feel it.

When you love your work people feel that too. So, you should love what you do and who you're doing it for but love because you genuinely care about them receiving the message, not just you receiving the paycheck. Love that you know your message can make a difference in someone's life. If you love people, you're going to want success for them in their life. So, if you show up and you love your audience, they will feel that and they will want more of that feeling. Then they will invite you back and they will tell their friends.

One of the greatest rewards of this business for me is I often get a phone call from someone who says, "I was given your card and told I had to hire you because you're amazing." Now when I get those calls, I do get a little nervous because that's a high bar. I am always hoping I can live up to it. However, it is such a compliment to know someone loved what I did enough to tell others to hire me.

I hope you love your work and your audience and get to experience those rewarding moments too. Mostly, I hope you love the difference you can make in someone's life. If you love the people you work with and the people you work for, know it will show and they will feel it. I encourage you to find a new way to show your clients love and see what rewards it has to offer.

M

Is for Motivation

WE MUST MOTIVATE OURSELVES BEFORE WE CAN MOTIVATE THEM

Now you may be thinking, "isn't motivation just a bunch of fluff and rah-rah stuff?" Maybe you've felt energized after listening to a motivational speaker but once you leave the room (or even a day, week, or month later) you don't actually remember what the presenter said.

Well, I love to motivate people. I love to inspire and encourage. However, I don't love it *that* much because motivation just leaves you fired up for a minute or a day or a moment. Yes, I am a motivational speaker but I'm also an activational speaker. Not only will I get you excited and bring you hope and belief and encouragement, but I'm also going to give you action steps to put to work and apply.

So, what is motivation without implementation? Well, it simply doesn't work. We need to have action steps and the strategy to get from where we currently are to where we want to go. Sometimes speakers will pass out candy bars and give us beautiful things to get us fired up but when we walk away, we don't remember them.

I had the privilege of experiencing something quite amazing. I was at a conference and I ran into this gentleman that said to me, "Annie, you probably don't remember me but two and a half years ago you spoke at a group I was at. You were amazing. I always dreamed of being a speaker. I watched your energy, your passion, your connection and I was so inspired." Now, he said this to me about midway through the conference. So, at the end of the conference, I went up to him and I said, "Hey, I'm sorry, can you tell me what was so inspiring about my speech?" He literally repeated back to me line for line the things that I had taught him to implement into his work life and his family life in the week to come. That's powerful. That's not just motivation. Motivation is great but if you don't show someone how to do it, sure, they'll be motivated but they'll forget.

As speakers, we have to motivate *and* encourage our audiences. We have to give them a process to get to where they want to go. So, if you're a motivational speaker, that's not just fluff, we need more motivation, encouragement and morale boosting in this world. However, you have to be able to give your audience the steps to apply that motivation and carry it into action. Also, make sure you inspire and encourage from an authentic place of how you live out your own life.

I hope you are motivated every day to take care of yourself so that you can do the good work that you are called to do. Whether that's speaking or growing a business or working for someone else. You will have greater success when you yourself are motivated and live out that motivation through action steps.

N

Is for Never Say Never!

NO ONE KNOWS WHAT THE FUTURE HOLDS

Do you ever find yourself saying "I'll never do that," or "that will never happen to me," or "my kids would never do that?" I've said those statements plenty of times and every time, you guessed it, those "things" happened to me. So be careful when you say "never" statements.

As soon as we say "never," it opens us up to "what if." "What if I have to walk through that?" or "what do I do in that circumstance?" I believe that people think they're going to quit from the first adversity they're faced with. If you don't expect there's going to be challenges and adversity when growing a business, well then, maybe you shouldn't be in business. Now, I don't like to say "never", but hear me out; never ever quit. Of course, there's times you will *have* to quit, but try changing your mindset to "I'm not going to quit. I might take a break when I get overwhelmed but then I'm going right back to work."

There's a million people out there selling us on a secret formula to be successful, to gain things in our life. Anything from books to coaching to programs. I don't think the secret formula is such a secret. Simply put, it's about working hard. It's about not letting the results of one day define what you're going to do the next day. It's about going to work even when you're tired, even when it's challenging, because hard work truly pays off. Yes, we should always work smart, but we should also always hustle and work hard. It's not going to come easy. Any person who has had great success in life will often say that it didn't come easy for them but quitting wasn't an option when things got hard.

So, are you going to quit, or are you *never* going to let people's opinions define what success means for you? Don't give up. Keep working hard.

Remember, never say never and never give up. Always believe in yourself and keep living the exceptional life you've always dreamed of.

0

Is for Opportunity

OPPORTUNITY TO SHOW KINDNESS

I was recently visiting my son in another state. While we were dining out, I thought to myself, "This restaurant has fabulous service, from the hostess to the busser." Each member of the staff, whether they were running out warm rolls or iced tea, they served us with a smile and encouragement.

As we were leaving the restaurant, I walked up to the hostess station and I asked to see the manager. Her face changed from having a smile to worry, wondering she had done wrong.

The manager reluctantly came out, also wondering what they have done wrong. Instead of complaining about something, which I think is a lot easier for us to do sometimes, I said, "I want you to know that my service tonight was amazing. The hostess greeted me with a smile and offered me my choice of tables. The waitress took our drink order right away and the bartender brought them over quickly. Other staff ran out warm food and warm muffins. The busser smiled at us. I want to thank you for this opportunity. I want to thank you for this time with my son that was so enjoyable with a great meal and excellent service."

In that moment, not only did the manager smile but the hostess also lit up with a smile. I wondered when the last time was that somebody stopped to ask to speak to the manager to say something kind.

The most rewarding moment for me was my son standing behind the hostess hearing me encourage others—the young people around us that sometimes we don't even see, let alone encourage, we take for granted.

Often, we are quick to complain when something doesn't work. When was the last time you thanked people for going above and beyond for a basic service? I encourage you to use your words to be kind and encouraging to those around you. Look people in the eye. Thank them for their great service.

P
Is for Passion, and Purpose

PAIN+PASSION = PURPOSE

I believe if you're not passionate about something, if you're just doing it because you seem like it will get you rich or it's the next best thing to do, people will sense that, they'll feel it. However, if it is your passion to do whatever work you're called to do, especially if you have a message to share—not just to teach your own story but teach the lessons you learned through your story—well, that will show up as well.

When you have a passion and it becomes your purpose, people will lean in to listen. They'll start to ask themselves "what am I passionate about? What is my purpose?" If we deliver an excellent message, they will feel that and they'll be driven to spend time digging into their passion and purpose. I know, so many people talk about passion and purpose but so few people *actually* know what that is. They give you the first answer they think of, but that's not always the truth. It's not always the right answer, not that there's a wrong answer. It's about discovering; taking time to discover what your passion and what your purpose is.

All of us at one time or another go through pain in our lives —sometimes physical, emotional, mental, financial, sometimes the inconvenience of a person that's difficult to work with. Whatever that pain is in your life that fuels you and gives you energy, it starts to absorb into your body whether you mean for it to or not. That pain, that irritation, it starts to fill up your body with frustration and stress giving you tension in your neck or your belly. It's on your mind, keeping you up at night. When that pain creates energy in your body and affects you, I believe that's your passion. Now what you choose to do with that passion is up to you. If you choose to use that passion for good and be a difference maker in the world— change the world or at least change the circle of the world that you live in—that becomes your purpose.

You could also use that passion, that energy, that

stress within you to be bitter, to be negative, to blame other people, to fill your life with excuses for why nothing works out for you, to feel sorry for yourself. You see all of us have reasons why we could feel sorry for ourselves or why we could be bitter. I just choose to use that fuel for good. It becomes my purpose.

What if you could teach people how to be more positive? What if you could teach people how to live by choice? What if you could teach people to stop blaming others or letting excuses define them? What would that look like? What would that feel like? When you work in whatever business you work in with passion and purpose in a positive way, well, that changes everything. And that game changer will not only affect your life and how you show up, but it will affect the people around you in a positive way.

So when you're ready to start a business or to grow a business and you choose to be successful, ask yourself "why am I so passionate about this? What is the purpose for me to do this work? What is it about this good work that matters to me? What difference will it make in other people's lives?"

Q

Is for Quality

NOT QUANTITY AND NOT QUICK—QUALITY

Delivering quality of whatever it is you deliver matters the most. Sometimes people will have a competition and I'll overhear "how many times did you speak this year?", "well how many times did *you*?" For some people speaking 200 times a year is not uncommon, that's their average. For some, their average is 100. For others, it's 50 or 20. I don't believe it's about how many times you speak or how big your audience is. I believe it's about the quality of what you deliver. Whoever you deliver it to—small, medium or large audience—they all deserve a quality presentation.

Don't be so quick to book the next client that you

don't pay attention to the present. Be present with the clients you're working with, whoever that is. Sometimes we're so quick to get through that sale so we can get the next one that we lose the quality because we're more focused on the quantity. If you want to be successful in business and be sustainable over the long haul, make sure you're delivering quality every single time—a quality presentation, quality presence when you're there, quality in what you do and why you do it. Deliver the best service and the best products so that your customer feels in that moment, whether they're paying $100 or $10,000, that they are worth it. I believe when you deliver quality service to your customers is when you get repeat business.

When I was in a different season in my life, when I was a single mom, I wouldn't always get quality customer service. People would look at me and they would think, "Oh she can't afford this." The truth is the first house I bought my Realtor didn't give me quality customer service. But the second house I bought, that Realtor whether I would have spent $10,000 or $10 million, I watched her with all her clients delivered the same excellent customer service.

I love to work with financial advisors that say to

me, "I'll work with a broke college student because I want to deliver my quality and my knowledge no matter what they have to give me." Now there are others who that have said that, I've watched them over the years then receive when that student gets an inheritance and they still work with them.

The next time when you find yourself thinking about how to be successful in sustaining your business, remember to always deliver the best quality, no matter the size of your customer's pocketbook.

R

Is for Relationships

RELIBLE RELATIONSHIPS CHANGE EVERYTHING

Value, value, value your relationships. You see, sometimes people qualify a person before they value them or not. Can they give me something? Can they do something for me? What will I get out of it? How much money do they make? How much money are they worth?

I believe that if you value relationships of those you've had the privilege of interacting with, then you're going to get more out of your business. When you value a relationship, you're telling that person that they matter more than the sale and getting to know them matters more than if you get the business.

What I have found and know, not only

personally but from working with thousands of people, is when you value relationships, not only do people feel that, but they appreciate that. They'll remember that and they'll test it. When you own a business people can get nervous that you're going to sell them all the time.

The greatest relationships are when they know you have something to offer. The key, though, is not to offer. Let them ask you. And if they never asked, that's okay too. Value the relationships. When you're sincere and valuing people for who they are—not for what they can do for you—people will feel that, and they'll want to be around you.

When I was President of the National Speakers Association (NSA) Minnesota Chapter, I often got phone calls and emails from people who were curious if they should get involved. Unfortunately, one of the first questions was, "What will it do for me? Will I get more business? Will I get referrals?" I tell them "No, but you will get education and a community."

Now, a side benefit to building those relationships and showing up and giving back is that occasionally people will say to me, "Hey, Annie, I have a speaking engagement I can't do, would you be interested?" I never became a part of

NSA for what I could get, but instead for what I could give.

Who could I be around? How could I give back to this community that I care about that's been there to support me and educate me on my journey to becoming a successful motivational keynote speaker? And because of that, I want to give back.

When people are looking for "what's in it for me," they lose the fact that just being there, you might gain a relationship, maybe even a friend, maybe even a lifelong friend. The speaker world is such a beautiful world because we understand each other's businesses, which is unique to other businesses. It's a great place to build community and connections.

I believe people are so quick to look for that sale that they forget that it's about the relationship. Take time to get to know people that you meet, find out about their families, their hobbies, their interests, find out if they like to go to the theater, maybe you love that too. You see, when you start to look at relationships as a gift, an opportunity for a friend, well, that's even more valuable than a sale. However, if you don't value your relationships, if you're insincere, you may get the sale but it won't last. They won't refer you. They'll know that you were insincere, that it was all about what you could get out of it rather than what you could give.

If you want to sustain success, genuinely care about the people you meet and build lifelong relationships. Ultimately it will reward you, but don't do it for the reward. Do it because you care about them and you want to give to them and connect with them. Eventually they may want to connect with you too.

Sustaining relationships, connecting and being intentional about them is how you create success and sustainability as a business owner.

S

Is for Story

WHAT'S YOUR STORY?

We all have a story and our story matters. If you're a speaker you better have a great story to teach, especially if you're doing a keynote. Your story, or someone else's story, connects people and stories sell and facts tell. So you need a story to connect with people. But it's more than that. There is a book inside of each of us. Whether or not we ever write it is up to us. You *do* have a story inside of you?

When I meet people they tell me "I want to write a book. I have a great story." Though they may have a great story, as many people do, it is not their story that's always the most successful in selling. It is the stories that we have lived and learned from that we teach others. So if you want to write your story, through a speech or through a book, make sure that you teach the lessons. How did you learn from it? How are you still applying it today? How has it helped you, personally and professionally, to be more successful in life? Share your stories, but don't forget to include those lessons. If you're telling a story because you're selling a product, make sure to tell us how you used the product? Why did you use the product? What were the results? What is your story around the product? Did it make you better at something? Did it make you stronger, brighter, more successful?

What do you do with that story? When I tell people about my book *Be the Exception*, I share stories of how people have responded when they read it. People that told me they never read but they started reading my book and they couldn't stop. People that told me they read it and as a result they'll never yell at their grandkid again because they realize nothing really matters enough to raise their voice, some have said they've changed their language or their attitude. They've stopped blaming other people and they've eliminated some of their skewed excuses and negative self-talk.

You see, stories are what sell products but stories also connect people—head and heart. If you only speak about logic, you only connect to the head. Though people may learn something, they may not remember who taught it to them. If you can connect the head (the logic) with the heart, then you'll make a connection and more than likely you'll make a sale.

If you want to sustain a successful business remember to connect stories to your products and your services.

T

Is for Time

TIME IS ALWAYS MOVING FORWARD, HOW ARE YOU SPENDING YOUR TIME

How much time do you have? Sometimes I tell audiences, "I'm so lucky, I get 36 hours in the day." They laugh, but what I'm really saying is I get a lot done. I think you can too. People will tell me they don't have enough time. In fact, time is one of the number one excuses of why people don't do things. Number one, we all have the same amount of time and if we value something enough we will make time for it Even if that means getting up at 4:00am so we can have quiet time or time to exercise.

Time is something we all have. The same

amount of time each day. Some of us die in our 40s or 60s or 80s, or even into our 100s. We don't know how much time we have in this lifetime. We do know we have the same amount of time in every day. So, the first question is, how will you use that time?

The second thing about time is that it takes time to grow a business. I know in my first year of business, here's my secret, I was in the hole for $40,000. The next year I broke even. I felt like I was winning because to go from negative $40,000 to a positive balance felt pretty good. I'll tell you that every year since I've doubled that and I'm doing quite well today. But I don't tell you that to gloat. I tell you that to say give yourself some time. Don't get up one day and think you're going to make $1 million or $100,000 or $50,000 or $500,000, whatever your number is, overnight. Know that it takes time to grow and sustain a successful business.

In the beginning, I had to invest in growing a business and creating a business and building a business in. All of that took time and money. I almost think that time is more valuable than money. When someone asks me to come spend time with them or to come look at something that they want to sell me, I have to first ask myself not just about the money but am I willing to spend an hour learning and listening.

Make sure that whatever you offer is valuable enough that people will spend their time investing with *you*, listening and learning from you, and that you have the right lessons to teach for their benefit, again, not for yours.

How will you use your time today? As a business owner, working by myself it's easy. I'm the boss, I can decide how much time I want to spend on my business and how much I want to spend time relaxing or going to lunch or coffee. I used to go to coffee all the time, all day long. One coffee would turn into three hours and two coffees a day would take up six hours and I would get nothing done. I had to learn to limit that time and go less often. I had to learn to be on time. I also had to learn to honor my time and not just spend a day chatting.

Owning your own business has lots of privileges. If you don't use your time wisely, you won't be successful. The more I dig in and actually work on my business when I'm not on the road traveling and speaking, the more successful my business is. Time is something you must manage and use wisely.

Be sure to take care of yourself. If you like to get up early to do something for yourself—quiet time or exercise—prepare for it that day. Set your working hours. For me, it's 8:00am-4:00pm, Monday through

Friday. Even without a boss, I will work those hours at minimum and occasionally on the weekends and evenings. Maybe in the beginning you're working a lot of hours, maybe 60 to 100 hours a week. Are you willing to put in that kind of time? Working for yourself has advantages and disadvantages.

One very important piece of being successful is managing your time and being dedicated, focused, and disciplined to make the phone calls, the outreach, and the follow up that you need to do to sustain a successful business.

U̅

Is for Unique

WHEN YOU STOP TRYING TO FIT IN AND EMBRACE YOUR UNIQUE SELF, YOUR AUDIENCE WILL LEAN IN

What does unique mean? It means to *be you*! Bring the best of you, the messy parts of you, all of you, when you go deliver. When you deliver a product or service, people buy from *you* more than they buy your product or service. Anybody can buy anything online. If you are the differentiator, you make them feel special, feel heard, empowered, encouraged, more successful, you bring them hope. Being unique is about bringing the best of *you*.

Embrace the messy. The reason I say that is because once I learned to do that, I embraced my messy parts. I'm not the world's greatest speller but I'm great at encouraging people. You see, when I bring them the truth of who I really am, my unique self, people get to know that and they either like it or they don't, but at least they know they're liking me. I believe that sometimes in the world we do so much harm to our business by comparing ourselves to other people and trying to emulate someone else, we get so obsessed with watching their videos, speaking like them, following their words and their actions, we lose part of ourselves. When your unique gifts and talents and even messy parts show up, people feel more connected to you and therefore feel more successful in the relationship with you.

In being my unique self, I would identify with a butterfly. Then for a while I identified with a unicorn. I thought I am a unicorn and people would call me a unicorn. But I thought, I'm so different than everyone else. I'm kind of weird. I'm kind of quirky. I'm kind of silly. I'm super passionate. I'm maybe too optimistic or unrealistic, but it's who I am. Recently I've decided I'd rather identify with a pineapple than any butterfly or unicorn. Stay tuned as I pass on my unicorn to a friend and instead engage in my new vision of being a pineapple.

I hope other people will be a pineapple, not to be

like me, but because they embrace the principles of a pineapple life. That it becomes part of who they are. Whatever is unique about you, whatever object makes people think of you or brand you, become that. Be the unique, successful version of yourself and people will show up to not just buy but to buy from you and your unique self.

CELEBRATE THE WINS EVERY DAY

Often, we wait for that big, huge victory before we celebrate, before we get excited, before we give ourselves credit for doing well. I'd love to encourage people to celebrate the little victories along the way. Did somebody answer the phone that's been ignoring you for a while? Did somebody have a conversation with you and *actually* noticed something you did well?

You see, when we celebrate the little victories along the way it keeps us motivated to keep going instead of waiting until we *actually* cross the finish line. I believe that sometimes we get so caught up in the big prize that we don't celebrate along the way. If we don't celebrate along the way, it's so easy to get discouraged because it takes time to get to that full victory.

The other day, I was having a gathering of people and somebody said to me, "I watch you and what you do. How you always open your house and you're always engaging. I so appreciate that." This was about my National Speakers Association (NSA) chapter and how I was serving. She was saying, "I love what you do for this chapter." Serving as the NSA Minnesota chapter president at the time, it was so wonderful to hear somebody recognize all the different things that I had done along the way instead of waiting to the end of the year leaving me thinking, "did I do this right?" I wasn't *looking* for that, but I really celebrated it. I remember that night during dinner I told my family that somebody really noticed all the extra effort I was making as the chapter president.

Celebrate the victories along the way. Don't wait until you finish the project or get the big sale. Celebrate the victories and allow people to celebrate you when you're successful. Even if you're not hitting the mark, if you're getting a little bit closer every day, celebrate that. The victories small and large will keep us going so we can sustain a successful business. I wish you all the best and many victories in the years to come.

W

Is for Way

KNOWING WHICH WAY YOU ARE HEADED MAKES IT EASIER TO GET THERE

What's the way to get it done? What is the way to be successful? Here's the truth. There's a lot of ways. There's not one right way to win the business. That's why I went through a whole ABC series because I think there's a lot of things involved in being successful and sustaining a successful business.

For me, as a speaker, sometimes I hear people say, "you have to get a book before you speak." "You have to speak to large audiences." "You have to charge this much." "You have to become a coach." It's not true. There are a lot of ways to find success.

How you define success and how you find success are the important things. First, ask yourself, what works for me? How do I want to be successful? How many times do I want to speak in a year? How many sales do I need in a month? How much money do I need to make? How do I want to earn that income? Is there one way? Is there 10 ways? Do I just want one business? Is speaking my main objective here? Is it coaching and consulting? Is it my books or my online course? Is it live events where I do retreats and gather people for a weekend? Is it a one-hour keynote to kick off a conference?

There's no right or wrong way to do your speaking business? It's more of a question-and-answer, trial-and-error. What works for you? I find that my sweet spot is keynoting about 50 times a year. I keynote a conference, open it up with energy and passion. I give them some framework to look forward to what's coming next. And then I can stay connected with that community or stay at the conference to connect with other people. I do offer coaching, but I don't sell it much. I have books and an online course. But those are all a small part of my business. My primary business is me speaking from the stage. It's not everybody's primary business. Ask yourself, where's my sweet spot? Is it selling books and that gets you booked once or twice a year?

One thing, especially with young parents that are starting to consider speaking, people tell me they want to travel and they want to do this or do that. I tell people, and I think it's really important, don't sacrifice your family for your dream of this business. Your spouse/partner and your kids need you around. Traveling will come. Maybe for that first season your primary work is through webinars or online courses. Maybe it's through books. I'm so grateful that my husband and I, while raising our kids, both spent the majority—80%+—of our time at home. We didn't miss a ski race, or a soccer tournament, or a dance recital. That was rewarding for us but also super rewarding for our kids to trust that we'll be there.

So, if you are looking to build a speaking business, start out at home. Don't sacrifice those years with your family. There will be plenty of time to go out and teach what you've learned. In fact, you might accrue some more lessons if you spend time at home during those years of raising the kids and being with your spouse or partner. Wait a little bit for those traveling years. If it doesn't fit into your schedule, don't try to fit the travel into your life. Instead, fit your life into your business. One of the greatest gifts of owning our own business is figuring that out. There's no one way to be successful. There are many ways. Ask yourself, does this work for me? Does it work for my family? Does it work for my plan to sustain success for the long haul? Figure out what you can do to be successful and sustain it. Look at other people's models. Ask yourself, what are you looking to do and where are you looking to do it. Trust me, there's plenty of work out there.

Professional speaker Walter Bond came to the National Speakers Association Minnesota chapter to speak. He said, "I grew a million-dollar speaking business in Minneapolis before I started traveling all around and speaking." Don't assume that you have to go far away or be gone a lot in order to be successful. You can do it at home wherever you live.

There are many ways in order to slice a pie. In this case, the pie will be successful and sustainable if you do it the right way for you. Think about it, prepare for it, plan for it, and then get out there and get to work so you can be successful in whatever your business is.

$$\overline{X}$$

Is for X-ray

LOOK BEYOND THE SMILE TO KNOW THE TRUE STORY

I believe an X-ray is about your truth. It's about looking on the inside. You see, sometimes people show up and they're fake or passive aggressive.

When I meet people and they're trying to sell something they don't believe in, I can feel that. I can sense it. If they're trying to sell themselves and they don't even believe in themselves, I get that gut feeling. Do you?

The X-ray is about knowing your truth, what you believe in what you stand by, and then going out and selling that. I love to sell hope because I believe in hope in all circumstances—the challenging ones, the interesting ones, the overwhelming ones. I still believe there's hope. Even if you've had a lot of no's, I know there's still a yes out there for you.

An X-ray is about looking inside and asking yourself and asking questions. Do I love this company? Do I love this work, this product, this service? If you love it, it'll be so much easier to sell. Look inside and ask yourself the hard questions because if you're just getting up every morning and going through the grind and you don't like or believe in what you're doing, it just gets harder. So many people get sick on Sunday nights because they don't believe in what they're doing.

Ask yourself, "what can I do that can pay the bills that I really believe in and allows me to sleep well?" Maybe you'll make less money, but maybe you'll find more joy? Isn't happiness more important than a big paycheck? Do what works for you. Be honest with yourself about who you are, what you teach, and what you love. You don't have to shout it from the rooftops but at least know it for yourself.

So, examine yourself and get an X-ray vision of your truth. Then go out and be successful in sustaining your business.

Y

Is for YOU

THERE IS ONLY ONE YOU, THE WORLD NEEDS YOUR STORIES, LESSONS AND DREAMS

When I meet speakers, I realize we all kind of talk about the same thing—just a little bit differently with our own personal stories and our own personal research on the topic. Sometimes people get nervous and say, "You both talk about customer service. Why do you want to be their friend? They're your competition!"

Nobody's my competition. Not that I think I'm better than anyone. What I do know is, people buy *you*. They don't buy the topic. Yes, they might need a talk about change or customer service or team building or leadership, but they ultimately buy *you*.

Even if 10 of us line up all speaking on the same topic, the audience is going to decide which personality resonates with their employees. They're going to decide which message feels like a good fit for them. They're going to decide whether or not they like *you*—sorry, but it's the truth. They're going to decide if they find you interesting or boring, too serious or too silly.

Don't worry if somebody talks about a similar topic as you. Ultimately, we all do. Instead, show up as the best version of yourself with your passion, your heart, your why. Then show up as *you* and deliver an impactful message that can change them. You see, when you show up with the best version of yourself, they're going to choose *you*. They may not choose you today, but they may next year. Maybe they choose your best friend in the speaking business. That's ok. That's the right person for them at that time.

It's *you* that's the deciding factor. So be the best version of yourself. Be successful. Don't be afraid of someone else stealing your topic or your message. Deliver it from your authentic self—what you've learned, what you've experienced, what you've watched other people you care about experience— and they'll hire you.

If you want to be successful and sustain a business, then show up as the best version of yourself. Be exceptional and be *you*.

Z̄

Is for Zoo

DON'T LET ALL THE ANIMALS SCARE YOU; THEY ARE JUST TRYING TO FIGURE IT OUT ALSO

Do you ever feel like you're in a zoo? Running a business all by yourself—doing the sales, the customer service, the follow up, dealing with the rejection, hoping for the promotion, not getting the gig then getting gig and then they ask you to stay longer, or to shorten that speech, or maybe lengthen it.

I was booked to deliver a 60-minute speech. I was going to kick off the event and I was so inspired. When I got to the event, my client said, "Any chance you could do 90 minutes? We really need to fill in some cracks. Somebody didn't show up."

You see, sometimes you just feel like a monkey in a zoo swinging from one branch to the next. From one project to the next, one town to the next. Then sometimes you just get in a rhythm and you think, I don't mind being an animal. I'm a lovable animal. I'm an encouraging animal. I'm a little goofy like a monkey.

As a business owner you juggle a lot of things. If you just embrace the beauty of the zoo, embrace all the differences and all the different interactions you'll have with all sorts of different people and different personalities—some huge and some small, some sweet and some aggressive—then you can love this business that we call being a professional speaker.

Sometimes I feel like a zoo but when I embrace the beauty of the zoo, the different colors, shapes and sizes of people that I engage with and interact with, it feels like the most beautiful place on Earth. Yes, it might feel overwhelming and loud at times. It might feel too colorful or too strong to manage it all. Take a deep breath, embrace the beauty, and keep moving forward.

Annie Meehan-CSP is an enthusiastic keynote speaker and author who inspires, enlightens, and energizes her audiences with a clear message that spurs listeners to break counterproductive patterns and **Be the Exception!**

As a keynote, Hall of Fame speaker, she has presented to numerous corporations, associations, and non-profit organizations, providing actionable strategies to strategically manage change, recognize the enormous power of words, and eliminate excuses that keep people from attaining their goals.

Her passion and charisma engage people in new and exciting ways, which inspires people to seize a more enriching and fulfilled path forward.

An expert on living an exceptional life, Annie has authored five additional motivational books. She has three adult children and lives in Fort Myers Beach, Florida with her husband, Greg. She loves volunteering in her community, traveling with her family, and walking (or being walked) with her two dogs, Peanut and Leo!

To learn more about Annie and her work, contact here at:

www.AnnieMeehan.com
Annie@AnnieMeehan.com

SPEAKING TESTIMONIALS

"The greatest gift I gave to the audience at our recent conference was having Annie as the opening keynote. She imbued such an incredibly positive and hopeful vibe among the attendees that it lasted the entire 2-day event. Annie is a class-act, a spark plug, a ball of energy, and a love letter all wrapped up in a tiny package..."

Joe Webb
President, DealerKnows

"Annie Meehan recently spoke at an event focused on women for our firm. She was outstanding - one of the best speakers I have ever seen. She made us laugh, made us cry and more importantly made us think. A great message of telling ourselves the right story and taking care of ourselves and others. I would highly recommend Annie to speak at any group."

Ryan J Kramer
Managing Partner
Northwestern Mutual Chicagoland

"...Annie brings hope to her audience through practical skills, storytelling, and personal awareness. She becomes part of the audience, and not just while on stage, but forever. Unlike many speakers you can hire to "deliver" a "speech", Annie engulfs herself with your group and bonds with people. She creates relationships and continues to mentor, educate and inspire for days, weeks and months after her stage performance is over..."

Pamela Shepherd
The Global Event Team

"Annie is a phenomenal speaker. Her presence is so positive, friendly and approachable. She was the keynote at our tech company's first annual client event and she was a perfect fit. I highly recommend Annie for any kind of speaking engagement or conference. We can't wait to work with our new friend Annie again!"

Angie Heck
IT Project Manger

ALSO BY ANNIE MEEHAN - CSP

Paths, Detours and Possibilities: A Journal to Map Out
Your Legacy

Be the Exception... Your 7 Keys to Transformation

Be the Exception... Bible Study

Be the Exception... Gratitude Journal

Pineapple Principle

Bruised to Beautiful... Life Lessons from Bananas

Choose to Soar... Navigating Disruption in Business
and Life

NOTES